W9-BHZ-888

Pack & Go

by Joy Dickerson

Pack and Go
   by Joy E. Dickerson

Illustrations by Michael DiGiorgio, Phyllis Pollema-Cahill
Photography: p.6 © Vermont Division for Historic Preservation; p.7 © Richard
   Cummins/CORBIS; p.8 left © Vermont Division for Historic Preservation, right
   © Vermont Division for Historic Preservation; p.13 © Bettmann/CORBIS; p.14
   © CORBIS; p.18 © Walter Stricklin/Stock South/PictureQuest; p.20 © George D.
   Lepp/CORBIS; p.24 © Texas Parks & Wildlife Department; p.25 © Texas Parks &
   Wildlife Department; p.31 © Tom Bean/CORBIS; p.32 © Leslie Harris/Index Stock
   Imagery/PictureQuest; p.37 © Dave G. Houser/CORBIS; p.38 bottom © Kennan
   Ward/CORBIS, top © George D. Lepp/CORBIS; p.43 © Photograph courtesy of Durell
   Johnson; p.44 © Darrell Gulin/CORBIS; p.49 © Bettmann/CORBIS; p.50 © Catherine
   Kane; p.55 © Lee Snider; Lee Snider/CORBIS; p.56 © Photograph courtesy of
   Maryland Department of Natural Resources Carter Library; p.61 © Alain Le
   Garsmeur/CORBIS; p.62 © Bettmann/CORBIS; p.67 © Philip Gould/CORBIS; p.68
   © Bettmann/CORBIS

Nonfiction Reviewer
   John Barell, Ed.D.
   Educational Consultant, The American Museum of Natural History
   New York City

Design, Production, and Art Buying by
   Inkwell Publishing Solutions, Inc., New York City

Cover Design by
   Inkwell Publishing Solutions, Inc., New York City

ISBN: 0-7367-1785-4
Copyright © Zaner-Bloser, Inc.

All rights reserved. No part of this book may be reproduced or transmitted in any form or
by any means, electronic or mechanical, including photocopying, recording, or by any
information storage and retrieval system, without permission in writing from the Publisher.

Web sites have been carefully researched for accuracy, content, and appropriateness. However,
Web sites are subject to change. Internet usage should always be monitored.

Zaner-Bloser, Inc., P.O. Box 16764, Columbus, Ohio 43216-6764, 1-800-421-3018

Printed in China

04 05 06 07 (321) 5 4 3 2

TABLE OF CONTENTS

INTRODUCTION

What is the farthest you have been away from your home? It's not the distance you travel that's important. You can learn just as much from a trip to a local museum as you can from a trip around the world. You can also learn a great deal by studying monuments.

A monument is built or created to honor a person, place, thing, or idea. The monuments in this book are not the best-known ones. Those are easy to find and learn about. You will read about monuments you have never heard of before. These monuments, however, still represent important people, places, and ideas—and the occasional insect.

Pack and Go Tips for Travel

The tips below will help you get the most out of any place you visit. The place might be 1,000 miles away or a historic building in your own neighborhood.

1. Pick a place you'll enjoy! If you like to get involved, go to the Hollenberg Pony Express Station in Hanover, Kansas. There, you can try on period costumes and pretend to be a Pony Express rider. Maybe you'd prefer to walk quietly and soak up the atmosphere. In that case, the Charlotte Hawkins Brown Memorial in North Carolina might be just the place for you.

2. Make sure to pick a place that matches your physical abilities. For example, Natural Bridge in Montana requires climbing up steep, narrow trails. You can call to find out whether the site is open to people in wheelchairs or with visual or hearing problems. Wear comfortable shoes, no matter what.

3. Read about the places you will be visiting. The Internet is a good place to start. You can also find great background information at the library. Don't forget that things can change between the time a Web site or book is written and the time you go.

4. Make sure you know when the monument is open. There's nothing worse than pulling up to a closed gate after a long trip. Call ahead for the hours of operation. Also find out whether there is a charge to get in. Most state monuments are free. However, you wouldn't want to arrive at some of them, such as the Kentucky Horse Park, with empty pockets!

5. Check the weather. Find out the average temperature in the area when you'll be visiting. Check the forecast for the time of your trip.

6. Find out how much time it takes to see what you want to see. For example, you could see Hyde Log Cabin in Vermont in about 30 minutes. However, you might want to spend a whole afternoon in Battle Creek, Michigan, exploring places related to Sojourner Truth. Plan ahead so your trip isn't rushed.

7. Try new experiences. Maybe you'll like the new foods offered to you at Picuris Pueblo. Maybe the view from the top of Coquille River Lighthouse will be worth the climb. Having new experiences is what traveling is all about.

8. Expect—and welcome—the unexpected. You'll lose a coat or take a wrong turn, but don't let it get you down. Maybe you'll meet some new friends while you're looking for your coat. Maybe you'll find a great restaurant down that wrong road.

9. Give yourself a challenge. For example, decide to learn the names of three plants at every place you visit, or decide to try one new food every day. Challenge yourself to ask five questions at each destination.

10. Promise yourself to have a good attitude, no matter what you encounter.

Spiral Around the States

Below is a map of the sites in this book. You will start on the outside edge of the United States and spiral your way toward the middle. As you read, remember that each monument is important to the people of that state. By the time you reach the middle of the lower 48 states—Kansas—you'll appreciate the diversity and history of our great nation. Enjoy!

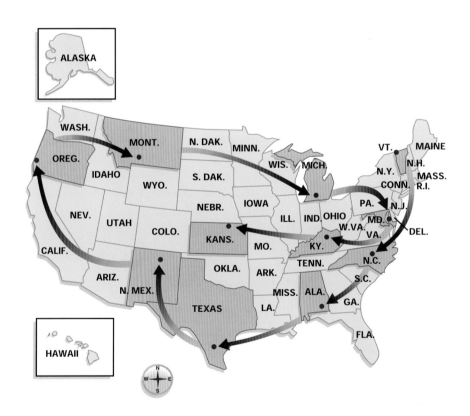

It's time to start your journey now! So, get ready! Get set! Get packed! GO!

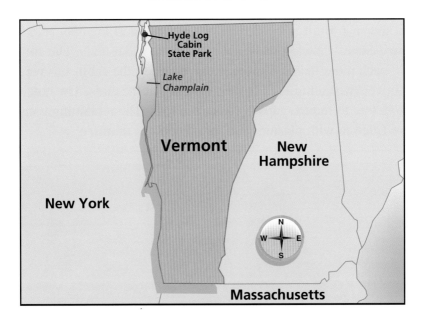

CHAPTER 1

Hyde Log Cabin
Grand Isle, Vermont

While a fire roars in the huge stone fireplace, an iron pot stands on three legs in the glowing coals. Potatoes and other vegetables bubble in the pot, filling the room with an aroma that makes your mouth water. The fire is the only light in the room. It casts flickering shadows over a table and chairs set for dinner with wooden plates. A spinning wheel stands nearby, waiting for skilled hands to draw out thread. The fire's heat barely reaches the far corner, where a bed with a leaf-filled mattress stands. Thick log walls keep out the worst of the cold.

Who do you think may have really lived this way? When you stand in the middle of Hyde Log Cabin, it's easy to imagine how the pioneers lived.

About the Cabin

When you visit Hyde Log Cabin in Grand Isle, Vermont, you visit the past. Built in 1783, it is one of the oldest log cabins in the United States. The log walls are made from cedar trees. The sturdy logs, each more than a foot wide, have helped the cabin survive for well over two centuries. They are notched at the ends. The notches fit together to reduce gaps between the logs. The remaining gaps were filled in with plaster, mud, or sometimes **manure**!

The Hyde Log Cabin State Historic Site stands on an island in Lake Champlain.

The cabin is only 25 feet long and 20 feet wide, smaller than most classrooms. In spite of this, the whole family lived in this room. The fireplace, used for cooking and heating, filled one end of the cabin. A loft was made by laying beams and boards across the tops of the walls. Up there, the young people and children in the family slept.

The Hyde Log Cabin became a Vermont Historic Site in 1945. The Grand Isle Historical Society then moved the cabin to a park. The society furnished the cabin with furniture from the late 1700s. This includes a bed, cradle, table, kitchen chairs, and a rocking chair. There are chests, boxes, and hooks for storage. A spinning wheel, cooking pots, and farm tools are placed where they would have been long ago. The cabin required major repairs in 1956. In 1985, the roof was rebuilt. Now it looks exactly as it did when the cabin was built in 1783.

As the pioneers moved west, they built and abandoned thousands of log cabins. Many looked just like this one. They had one big room, a large fireplace, and a loft.

Spinning wheels were used to make thread. The thread was used to make cloth for clothes and blankets.

Meet Jedediah Hyde

Long ago, Jedediah Hyde, Jr., and his family lived in this cabin. Jedediah was only 22 years old when he built it. By the time he turned 22, he had already served eight years as a soldier during the Revolutionary War. He had enlisted in the army of the brand new United States when he was just 14 years old.

In the army, Hyde learned **surveying**. Surveyors mark the boundaries of pieces of land. After the war, surveyors had lots of work. Many soldiers were paid with land, not money. Surveyors were sent into unsettled areas. They marked where one veteran's land ended and another's land began.

One place that Hyde and his father surveyed was Grand Isle in Vermont. Grand Isle is on an island in Lake Champlain. The Hydes found that many veterans wanted to sell the land they had been given on Grand Isle. The Hydes bought many of those parcels. Jedediah Hyde built his cabin on one of them. Members of his family lived in the cabin until the 1930s.

Cabin life centered on the fireplace, which was used to cook the food and heat and light the cabin. Supplying the fireplace with wood was a never-ending job. The children in the family were often responsible for chopping wood and gathering kindling.

Pack & Go

If you want to visit the Hyde Log Cabin State Historic Site, make sure to check your clock and calendar. The cabin is open only from Wednesday to Sunday from 11:00 A.M. to 5:00 P.M. It's also open only from July 4 through Labor Day. It costs $1 to get in. The weather is sunny and warm during the time the cabin is open. Wear jeans or shorts.

To get to the cabin, take U.S. Route 2 north from Burlington, Vermont. Route 2 takes you to the village of Grand Isle. The cabin is just north of the village. For more information about the Hyde Log Cabin State Historic Site, call (802) 828-3206. If you can't go to Vermont, there might be a park or museum nearby where you can see a similar cabin.

Other Sites and Activities

Are you going to Vermont to see the Hyde Log Cabin? While you're there, check out these other sites. For more information, call Vermont's Department of Travel and Tourism at (802) 828-3236.

- Learn about the people who lived in Vermont before Europeans arrived. Visit Chimney Point State Historic Site in Addison. A tavern from the 1700s has been turned into a museum. The museum covers 8,000 years of Native American history.
- Experience what life was like in the 1700s and early 1800s. Stop at the Shelburne Museum in Shelburne. It is a restored village. There, you can tour museums, gardens, and a paddle-wheel boat.
- Visit the birthplaces of two presidents. President Chester A. Arthur was born in Fairfield. His historic site is near the Hyde Log Cabin. President Calvin Coolidge's birthplace is in Plymouth Notch.
- Try to fit in some skiing. Vermont offers many opportunities for outdoor activities. In the fall, many people travel there to see the blazing colors of the maple trees. Vermont's many resorts offer a variety of activities for the summer months, as well.

CHAPTER 2

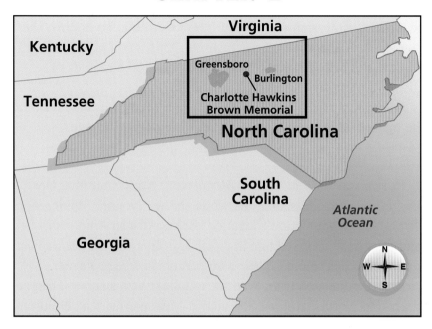

Charlotte Hawkins Brown Memorial
Sedalia, North Carolina

*"In a little white church, which was schoolroom and church combined," says she, "my life's work began. The plastering was broken and half of the windowpanes were out. With these crudities [sic] defects and its homemade log seats, it seemed to me a forlorn, forsaken place; and yet those fifty or sixty boys and girls, barefooted and **unkempt,** heartened me with their bright questioning eyes, and in a little while I forgot the isolation and hardships and lost my very soul in trying to help them."*

—Charlotte Hawkins Brown

From *Women Builders,* by Sadie Iola Daniel (Washington, DC: Associated Publishers, 1931).

Charlotte Hawkins Brown was describing her first days as a teacher. She dedicated her life to education. She wanted to help the African-American children of North Carolina. To do this, she founded the Palmer Memorial Institute. This was a private school in Sedalia, North Carolina. The school prepared hundreds of African-American students for college.

In 1983, the Charlotte Hawkins Brown Memorial State Historic Site opened. It is located at the Palmer Memorial Institute.

A Brief Biography

Brown was born in 1883 in Henderson, North Carolina. Her family moved to Massachusetts while she was young. Moving north allowed her to get a good education. Being African American, she would not have received one in North Carolina. Education was very important to her parents. Their own parents had been slaves.

Brown graduated from Wellesley College as a teacher. Then she returned to North Carolina. She taught African-American children at a missionary school. The school met in a one-room, run-down church. Brown was inspired by her eager students and their parents. She became a community leader. After only one year of teaching, all one- and two-room schools were closed. When Brown's school closed, she started her own school. In 1902, she opened the Palmer Memorial Institute. She named it after the person who had guided her own education. That was Alice Freeman Palmer, president of Wellesley College.

Running the School

The Palmer Memorial Institute was a boarding school. That means the students lived there. It was highly respected. More than 90 percent of its students went on to college.

Charlotte Hawkins Brown ran the school for 50 years, supporting education for all people. She also worked for **civil rights**

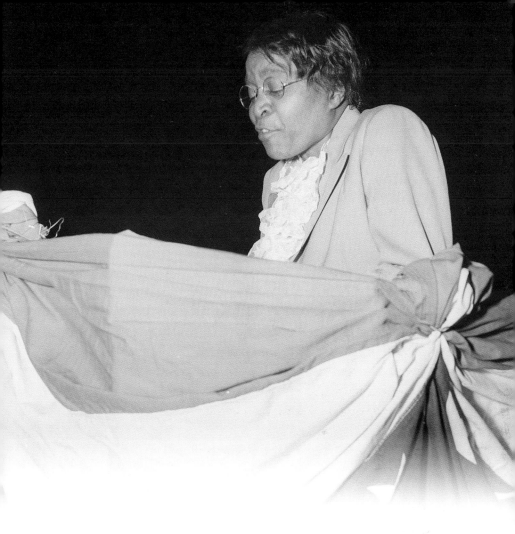

Charlotte Hawkins Brown (1883–1961) started as a teacher. She ended her career as president of Palmer Memorial Institute, the school she founded.

for African Americans. She even wrote several books. The great success of her students is a measure of her success.

Charlotte Hawkins Brown died in 1961. Her school closed in 1971—for a good reason. Partly thanks to her work, schools had become **integrated**. Both black and white students could now attend all public schools.

School Days

"When standing or sitting, hold yourself erect. Don't slouch. Talk clearly and sufficiently loud for everyone in the room to hear."
—Charlotte Hawkins Brown

These were just a few of Brown's guidelines. The students at her school had to meet high standards. In addition to school subjects, they were expected to learn good manners and proper behavior. They had to follow a strict dress code. Teachers were always present at social gatherings to encourage students to behave. Students also learned business skills by running the school's Tea House.

Students at the Tea House School

The Tea House still stands today.

In 1947, writer Griffith Davis visited the school. She wrote, "About the campus there is a certain air of culture … training begins at breakfast, with nine schoolmates who all practice the correct way to eat … there are classes until four. Then comes study, socializing, and chores. All students are assigned to do two hours' work daily at the school."

At the Memorial

North Carolina honored Charlotte Hawkins Brown with a memorial. She is the first woman and the first woman of color to be honored in this way. At the memorial, you can walk around the school Brown founded. The Visitor Center is located in the Carrie M. Stone Cottage. Tours of the school leave from there. The Visitor Center displays items that belonged to Brown and to students of the school.

The Memorial also houses a center. Its staff researches the contributions of other North Carolina African Americans. The Memorial encourages research into African-American history and culture.

Pack & Go

The Charlotte Hawkins Brown Memorial State Historic Site is open almost every day. However, between November and March, it is closed on Mondays. You can call (336) 449-4846 to find out the hours. Admission is free.

To get there, take the Rock Creek Dairy Road exit (Exit 135) on Interstate 85 between Burlington and Greensboro, North Carolina, to U.S. 70 and turn left. The institute will be on the left.

In the winter, the temperature here is in the low 50s. However, you should dress lightly in the summer. Average highs are in the upper eighties in July!

Other Sites and Activities

North Carolina has a beautiful coastline. It includes historic lighthouses and great beaches. The Wright Brothers took the world's first airplane flight in Kitty Hawk. To plan a trip, call the Travel & Tourism Department at (800) 847-4862.

You also might want to check these other historic sites:

- At the Reed Gold Mine State Historic Site, you can find gold! You can go down into a mining tunnel and pan for gold. You can also hike on nature trails. The Reed Gold Mine is in Stanfield.
- Town Creek Indian Mound is in Mt. Gilead. You can see a ceremonial center, temples, and burial huts. They were used by Native Americans from the Pee Dee culture. The Pee Dee lived in this area about 800 years ago.
- President James A. Polk was born in Pineville. Visit his birthplace and find out about his many accomplishments.

CHAPTER 3

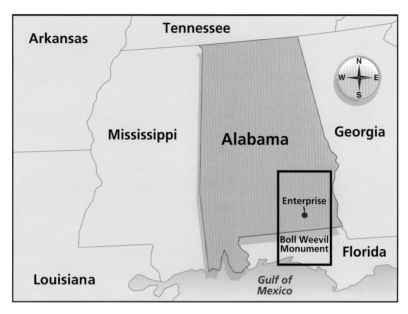

Arkansas

Tennessee

Mississippi

Alabama

Georgia

Enterprise

Boll Weevil Monument

Florida

Louisiana

Gulf of Mexico

N
W E
S

Boll Weevil Monument
Enterprise, Alabama

It's July 4, 1916. Most people in the United States are celebrating Independence Day. However, the farmers in Coffee County, Alabama, are worried. The local **economy** depends on cotton plants, but the plants are dying. Cotton buds drop from their stems. The round bolls—those that grow at all—are dried up instead of fat with cotton. If you cut open a boll, you see a sickening sight. Whitish, wormlike insects are chewing away at the plant. They are boll weevils. The people of Enterprise, the county seat of Coffee County, don't know what to do. How can the farmers fight the weevil?

Why did they end up building a monument to this destructive insect?

The Boll Weevil Monument rises more than 13 feet above the main street in Enterprise. It is a statue of a woman. She is holding something above her head. Look closer, and you will see that she is holding a bug—a boll weevil, to be exact.

Welcoming the Weevil

In 1915 and 1916, the boll weevil arrived in Alabama. As the cotton began to die, many towns suffered. John Pittman was the Coffee County extension agent. His job was to provide farmers with information that would help them farm. He urged them to try a new crop—peanuts.

C.W. Baston was one of the first to make the switch. He sold his peanuts for much more than others were earning from cotton.

Boll Weevil Monument, Enterprise, Alabama

More farmers changed to peanuts. The Enterprise Cotton Seed Oil Company stopped making cottonseed oil. Instead, it began to make peanut oil.

Honoring the Bug

Growing peanuts turned out to be a good idea. Coffee County farmers overcame their anger at the boll weevil. Instead, they felt grateful. That's why they built a monument to this bug. The monument was dedicated on December 11, 1919. More than 5,000 people attended. A sign next to the monument says, "In profound appreciation of the Boll Weevil and what it has done as the **Herald** of Prosperity, this monument was erected by the Citizens of Enterprise, Coffee County, Alabama."

Switching crops may not sound difficult. However, farmers in southern Alabama had always grown only cotton. It took courage for them to try something new. People in Enterprise are proud of the way they handled this crisis. Nearly a century later, the town still welcomes new ideas and businesses.

Meet the Boll Weevil

Boll weevils are beetles. They have long "noses" and small wings. They came from Central America and the West Indies.

When people began growing cotton in Mexico, the boll weevils showed up. They flocked to these huge fields for a free lunch. These beetles weren't native to Mexico, so they had no enemies there. Their population grew rapidly. By 1863, the weevils had caused much damage in Mexico. Farmers there stopped growing cotton. The weevils moved east and north at about 70 miles a year. By 1892, they were damaging cotton plants in Brownsville, Texas. By 1915, they made it all the way to Alabama.

1. In spring, female boll weevils leave their winter shelter and climb to the top of maturing cotton plants.

2. The weevil pierces the cotton boll with her snout and lays eggs inside.

5. Adult weevils leave the boll to seek winter shelter.

3. Eggs hatch in three to five days.

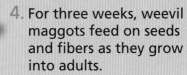

4. For three weeks, weevil maggots feed on seeds and fibers as they grow into adults.

Today, boll weevils are found everywhere cotton is grown in the United States. Fighting weevils is a major cost of raising cotton. Farmers destroy cotton stalks as soon as possible. That clears out the places where adult weevils spend the winter. They spray fields with pesticides. They change the time of planting. And they support research into types of cotton that can resist the weevils.

Pack & Go

You can see the Boll Weevil Monument any time. In fact, in Enterprise, it is hard to miss! The monument stands at the corner of Main Street and College Street. Enterprise is in southeastern Alabama, about 85 miles southeast of Montgomery. To get there, take U.S. Route 331 south to U.S. Route 84. Go east on Route 84.

Coffee County has mild winters and hot summers. You'll need only a light jacket in January. In July, you'll need shorts and sunscreen. Call the Enterprise Economic Development Corporation at (334) 347-0581 for more information.

Other Sites and Activities

While in Enterprise, tour the Boll Weevil Soap Company. There, soap is made from cotton and peanut oil. Visit the Little Red Schoolhouse, built like schoolhouses in the 1800s. Stretch your legs on the trails at Johnny Henderson Family Park. In April, you can see the Piney Woods Arts and Crafts Festival. Artists from all over the Southeast show and sell their work.

For more information about traveling in Alabama, call 1-800-ALABAMA. Here are some other places you might want to see there:

- The Fort Rucker Army **Aviation** Center is near Enterprise. Two monuments in the town honor army flyers. The **Aviator** Monument is at the corner of Park Street and Plaza Drive. "The Huey" Helicopter is in a local park. Look for the "Walk of Generals" around the base of the helicopter.
- The Civil Rights Memorial is in Montgomery. It honors people who lost their lives in the fight for civil rights, including Martin Luther King, Jr. The memorial features a beautiful fountain.
- Check out some musical sites. A museum in Montgomery documents the life of Hank Williams, Sr. His boyhood home is a museum in Georgiana. The Alabama Music Hall of Fame is in Tuscumbia. Musicians honored there include Emmylou Harris, Nat King Cole, and Lionel Richie.
- Tuscumbia is also the birthplace of Helen Keller. You can learn more about her there. See the play about her early life, "The Miracle Worker."

CHAPTER 4

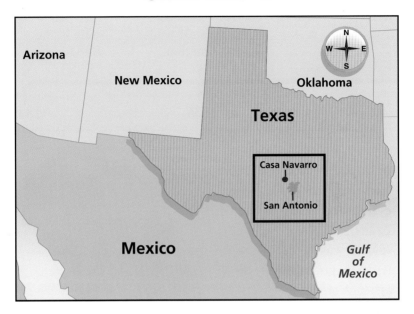

Casa Navarro
San Antonio, Texas

The Strongest Champion

Jose Antonio Navarro was born in San Antonio in 1795. During his life, he lived in four countries. Yet, he did not move more than a few miles. How did this happen? During Navarro's time, there were a lot of changes going on in this region. First, he was a citizen of a Spanish colony. After 1821, he lived in the Republic of Mexico. In 1836, he became a citizen of the Texas Republic. After 1845, he was a United States citizen.

Navarro was important in each of these changes. He was a state senator in the Mexican Republic, the Texas Republic, and the United States. He signed the Texas Declaration of Independence.

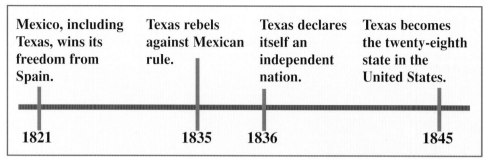

| Mexico, including Texas, wins its freedom from Spain. | Texas rebels against Mexican rule. | Texas declares itself an independent nation. | Texas becomes the twenty-eighth state in the United States. |

1821   1835   1836   1845

He helped write constitutions. He often wrote about the rights of the **Tejanos,** which is Spanish for Texans.

Navarro was a businessman, politician, and writer. A quiet man, he liked to keep his personal life simple. You can see that in the way Navarro lived his life and what was important to him. He was committed to supporting democracy and Mexican rights. In doing so, he helped shape history.

Navarro died at his home in 1871. He left a name that is honored and lived an admirable life, full of heroic deeds.

Jose Antonio Navarro

The Casa Navarro State Historic Site

Casa Navarro

Look at the time line. It shows how Jose Antonio Navarro's life was deeply connected with Texas independence and freedom. His home is called Casa Navarro. It has been made into a state historic site.

Navarro's House

Casa is the Spanish word for *house*. *Casa Navarro* means *Navarro's house*. The Casa Navarro State Historic Site includes three buildings. This is where Navarro spent the later years of his life. The buildings were built in 1848. Several rooms have been

restored. They were reconstructed so they look like they did when Navarro lived there.

One of the restored rooms is Navarro's office. It is furnished like it was when he was working there. When you enter the room, you can imagine Navarro at his desk. He might be writing a newspaper article. It might support the rights of Tejanos in the new Republic of Texas. Maybe he would be researching a point of law for the new Texas state **constitution**.

The neighborhood around the house is called the Barrio de Laredo. It was on the road to the city of Laredo. Navarro had homes outside of the city. However, he chose to live where the Mexican culture was strongest. Today, Barrio de Laredo is in the heart of downtown San Antonio.

Texas During Navarro's Life

Remember the Alamo? That important battle was fought in 1836. What was happening before 1836? Was Texas just empty land? Not at all! Texas history began centuries before the Battle of the Alamo.

Casa Navarro is in San Antonio, which was once a Native American village. Spanish soldiers arrived in 1718. They came from Mexico. At that time, Mexico was a colony of Spain. The soldiers built a fort and a church in the village. They called their settlement "San Antonio de Bexar." In time, many of the native people grew ill from diseases brought by the soldiers. A lot of them died. Slowly, the population of San Antonio became Mexican.

Road to Independence

In 1815, the people of Mexico rebelled against Spain. (Mexico still included Texas.) In 1821, the Mexican people won their freedom from Spain. In 1824, they set up a country modeled on the United States. Texas became a state of Mexico.

Soon, however, a **dictator** took over Mexico. He took away the people's freedom. By this time, Texas included many people from the United States. The people of Texas rebelled against the Mexican ruler. In 1836, Texans won their freedom from Mexico. They set up their own country.

In 1845, Texas joined the United States. Its Mexican residents were called Tejanos, which is Spanish for Texans. Many changes were occurring in Texas. Still, Navarro made sure that the Tejanos did not lose their rights.

Pack & Go

Casa Navarro is open Wednesday through Sunday. The hours are 10:00 A.M. to 4:00 P.M. The cost is $2 for adults and $1 for children under 12. Call (210) 226-4801 for more information.

The home is at 223 S. Laredo Street, San Antonio. It's across the street from the San Antonio Police Department.

It's warm all year round in San Antonio. Even in January, the average daytime temperature is in the middle sixties. In July, San Antonio is downright hot! Daytime temperatures are often 90 degrees or above. Be sure to pack your sunglasses!

Other Sites and Activities

Texas is our second largest state. It has a long, long list of things to do and see. Close to Casa Navarro, you'll find the Alamo. You can also see a restored Mexican village called La Villita. It shows what life was like in San Antonio in the 1800s.

To find out more about these sites and about other places to visit in Texas, call the Travel and Information Division at (800) 452-9292. You might ask for more information about these places:

- The birthplace of President Dwight D. Eisenhower is in Denison. This home has been restored. It looks as it did in 1890, the year when Eisenhower was born.
- The National Wildflower Research Center is in Austin. This center, founded by Lady Bird Johnson, promotes and protects wildflowers.
- Dinosaur Valley State Park is in Glen Rose. You can see some of the best-preserved dinosaur tracks in the world here. They are in the riverbed of the Paluxy River.

CHAPTER 5

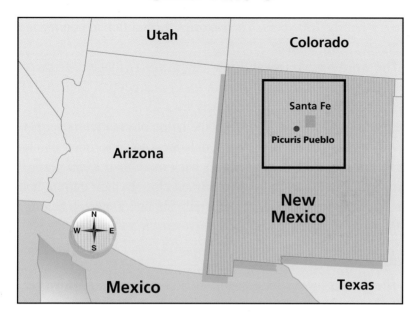

Picuris Pueblo
Penasco, New Mexico

It's December 20. There is no snow, but wind howls through the valley. It stirs fallen cottonwood leaves into flight. It churns dust into miniature tornadoes that beat against the buildings of Picuris Pueblo. The streets are deserted on the **winter solstice,** the shortest day of the year.

On this day, the people of Picuris stay quiet. They don't dance or sing. They don't make pottery, paint, or farm. Instead, they gather in the home of a storyteller. They eat, and they listen. Some of the stories are scary, while others are mysteries and fairy tales. Some tell the legends of Magpie Boy or Old Man Coyote. In this way, stories are passed from the older people to the younger people.

Picuris Pueblo rests in a valley of the Sangre de Cristo Mountains in northern New Mexico. The Picuris people have lived there for nearly 750 years. Their stories form a thread connecting the present with the past.

The word *pueblo* (**pwehb**•loh) can mean a village or town. It can also mean a group of Native American people. Sometimes it describes the buildings where they live.

Picuris (**pik**•uh•rees) Pueblo is the home of the Picuris people. *Picuris* means "painters." These people are known for their painting. The Picuris can trace their ancestors back more than 1,000 years. The ruins of ancient Picuris homes are buried close to their current home, near Penasco, New Mexico. Today, only about 350 people belong to the Picuris Pueblo. In the past, there were as many as 5,000.

Pueblo Revolution

The Picuris have a long history of self-government. However, in 1583, they were brought under Spanish rule. In 1680, the Picuris and other pueblos revolted, forcing the Spanish to flee. The pueblos kept out the Spanish for many years. However, the Spanish returned. The Picuris, as leaders of the revolt, were harshly punished. Many were killed. Much of their land was taken.

Still, the pueblo survived. Today, the Picuris Pueblo is part of the Eight Northern Pueblos. The group runs schools and a craft cooperative. The craft cooperative helps pueblo artists sell pottery, paintings, and weavings. Each year, the Eight Northern Pueblos Arts & Crafts Show is held. The show brings many tourists to the area.

Every July, Picuris Pueblo holds the High Country Tri-Cultural Arts and Crafts Fair. *Tri-cultural* means "three cultures." The show celebrates art from the three main cultures in New Mexico. They are the Anglo (white), Hispanic, and Native American cultures.

Picuris Pueblo—"the village of the painters"

Touring the Pueblo

At Picuris Pueblo, you can watch artists create pottery or paintings. You can visit the museum to find out how the Picuris lived in the past. You can tour the ruins of ancient pueblos and study prehistoric farming.

The Picuris Pueblo also holds traditional Native American festivals and dances. One example is the Sundown Torchlight Mass Procession in late December. It is followed by Picurisian Matachina Dances.

Picuris potter adding a coil

Shining Mica Pots

Most of the pueblos of Arizona and New Mexico have made pottery for thousands of years. Each pueblo makes a different kind of pot. The pots from Picuris Pueblo sparkle with mica, a shiny mineral in the clay near the pueblo.

To make a pot, the potters begin by digging clay from pits that have been used for generations. Then they grind the dry clay and take out any bits of rock or dirt. Next, they soak the clay in water. When the clay is ready, the potters knead it like bread dough.

Finally, it's time to make the pot. Picuris potters roll the clay into long, snakelike strips. Then they coil each strip into a circle, making a spiral. Each coil makes the pot a little higher. As they work, they pinch the rows of coils together, adding more coils until the pot is the right size and shape.

Next, Picuris potters may use corncobs to smooth the sides of their pots. They might also carve designs into them. When the pots are ready, they are put upside down in a fire pit. Bark is piled on top of them and set on fire. The heat from the fire hardens the clay, but many pots break in the firing pit. The pottery that survives sparkles brightly with mica from the clay.

Pack & Go

The Picuris Pueblo and its museum are open every day from 9:00 A.M. to 6:00 P.M. To find out about the cost of tours and other activities, call (505) 587-2957. You can hike, tour the ruins, eat traditional foods, and see live buffalo. Be ready to examine the beautiful arts and crafts. A fee is charged to take pictures.

The pueblo is about 24 miles southeast of Taos on Route 76. Taos is a world-famous arts community. Stop for a visit on your way to Picuris.

January high temperatures in this region are about 45 degrees. In July, it is seldom hotter than 80 degrees. If you'll be out after dark, take a coat. The temperature drops rapidly when the sun goes down.

Other Sites and Activities

New Mexico has mountains, deserts, rivers, and caves. Native American sites, both prehistoric and current, offer a wealth of arts and culture. Chaco Culture National Historical Park is one example.

To find out more about places to go in New Mexico, call the Department of Tourism at (800) 545-2040. Meanwhile, check out these locations:

- Explore the other pueblos in the Eight Northern Pueblos group. They are Nambe, Pojoaque, San Ildefonso, San Juan, Santa Clara, Taos, and Tesque. See if you can tell their styles of pottery apart.
- Tour the Very Large Array (VLA) radio telescope. The VLA is a group of 27 huge satellite dishes. They move together to gather radio signals from outer space. The VLA is in Socorro.
- At Living Desert State Park in Carlsbad, see desert species in their natural environment. You can tour a cactus greenhouse and explore a prairie dog town.
- While you're in Carlsbad, visit Carlsbad Caverns National Park. It includes one of the largest caves in the world. On summer evenings, you can watch hundreds of thousands of bats emerge from the caves. Don't worry: the bats live in a part of the caverns that is not open to the public. They are well protected from tourists!

CHAPTER 6

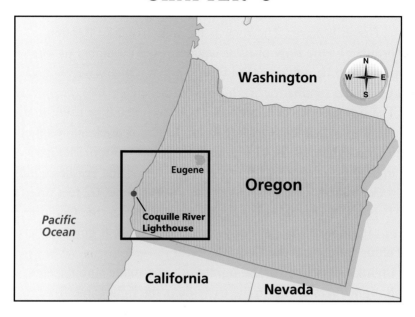

Coquille River Lighthouse
Bandon, Oregon

The small ship rolled in the crashing waves. White foam flew as waves broke over the deck. As clouds blotted out the moonlight, everything was black. It took all of the captain's and navigator's skills to keep the ship on course.

Here, off the coast of Oregon, the currents can be tricky even in calm water. Where the rivers meet the ocean, they form **sandbars** and change the way the water flows. That night, near where the Coquille River flows into the Pacific Ocean, the pilot needed more than skill. He needed help! He scanned the horizon, squinting against the spray. There it was—the gleaming light from the Coquille River Lighthouse. Using the beacon as a guide, he steered the ship safely into the mouth of the river and to the town of Bandon.

Spotlight on Coquille River Lighthouse

The Coquille (koh•**keel**) River Lighthouse stands at the mouth of the Coquille River. The river is the main route to Bandon. Unfortunately, the flow of river water caused a sandbar to form. Ships need to be guided around the sandbar. Otherwise, they would end up on the sandbar or crash onto the beach.

The Coquille River Lighthouse was completed in 1896. It stands on a tiny island called Rackleff Rock. Made of brick and painted white, the lighthouse is 47 feet high from base to top. The base of the lighthouse is about 15 feet above the water that crashes against the rocky island. That means that the light is about 62 feet up in the air. This is not very tall for a lighthouse. However, the Coquille River Lighthouse was perfectly suited for its job. It guided boats and ships safely into the Coquille River.

Lightkeepers lived at the lighthouse and made sure the light was lit all night every night. In the early days the light came from an oil lamp. Keeping the light lit meant making sure there was enough oil and keeping the wick lit. Even in the worst storms, the light shone. Sometimes the lightkeeper's whole family had to help keep it lit.

Restoring the Light

By 1939, new technology had replaced the lighthouse. The buildings were abandoned. The light was removed. After its windows were broken, water damaged the lighthouse. By 1970, Coquille River Lighthouse was shipwrecked!

Fortunately, the lighthouse was made a part of Bullards Beach State Park. Park staff worked many hours to restore the building. In 1991, a new solar-powered light shone from the lighthouse. Once again, it guided boats and ships into the river. Keeping the lighthouse ship-shape is a continuing battle. Many people contribute money to make repairs. Others donate their time. Some lead tours of the lighthouse during the summer.

The Coquille River Lighthouse today—a treasured reminder of the past

Spotting the Gray Whale

After you have seen Coquille River Lighthouse, stay awhile at Bullards Beach State Park. It offers miles of beautiful coastline where you can camp, hike, bike, and fly a kite. At Face Rock Wayside, you may catch a glimpse of a gray whale, especially early on a spring morning. Watch for a spout of water or a flipping tail. Gray whales travel in groups of two or three, so if you see one, look around for more.

Gray whales weigh as much as 40 tons and may be up to 50 feet long. That makes the gray whale longer than the Coquille River Lighthouse is tall!

Gray whales migrating along the West Coast, as seen from Bullards Beach State Park, where the Coquille River Lighthouse stands

An "Otter" Animal

Sea otters used to live all along Oregon's coast. Today, you are more likely to see a whale than an Oregon sea otter. You may be surprised to learn that anthropologists are working to solve the otter problem. **Anthropologists** study how ancient humans lived.

Long ago, the people of Oregon ate many sea otters. Anthropologists are collecting otter bones from ancient cooking fires. They study the bones. They want to find out whether these otters looked more like California otters or Washington otters. This knowledge will help decide which type of otter to release in Oregon. You may soon be seeing more sea otters in Oregon!

Pack & Go

You can visit the Coquille River Lighthouse all year round. Bullards Beach State Park is open from dawn to dusk. To tour the inside of the lighthouse, call ahead. The phone number is (541) 347-2209.

To get to the Coquille River Lighthouse, take Highway 101 north from Bandon, Oregon. The entrance to Bullards Beach State Park is on your right about a mile north of Bandon. If you cross the Coquille River Bridge, you've gone too far. Keep your eyes open on your way to see the lighthouse!

The coast of Oregon is cool and wet. The high temperatures in July reach only the low seventies. The winters are mild, with high temperatures in the low fifties, so you'll need a jacket. The coast gets lots of rain, so take an umbrella, too!

Other Sites and Activities

Most people think of outdoor activities when they think of Oregon. They think of forests and coastlines. They think of beaches and dune buggies. However, Oregon has some lively indoor activities, too. To find out more about Oregon's indoors and outdoors, call the Tourism Division at (800) 547-7842. Here are some activities to consider:

- Tour Dogs for the Deaf in Central Point. This organization trains dogs to help people who cannot hear. The training rooms look like rooms in homes. You can watch a training session and tour the kennels.
- Check out the Portland Art Museum in Portland. The collection of artwork spans 35 centuries! From ancient to modern, you're sure to find something you like.
- Visit the Air Center at the Redmond Airport. There, firefighters learn to parachute into fires.

CHAPTER 7

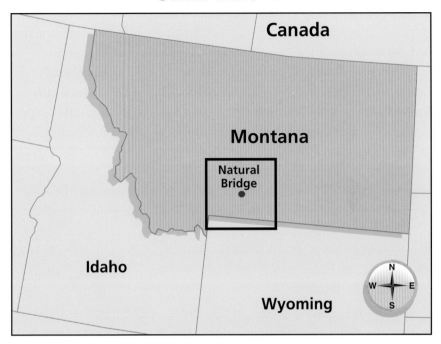

Natural Bridge State Monument
Big Timber, Montana

If a bridge falls into a river and no one is there to hear it, does it make a sound? You can argue about the answer, but between 6:00 P.M. on July 16, 1988, and noon the next day, a bridge did fall.

The bridge that fell was a natural rock bridge. It spanned a scenic waterfall in the Boulder River near Big Timber, Montana. When the Johnson family passed by on the evening of July 16, the bridge was still there. When Dorothy Hansen and her family arrived the next afternoon, it was gone. No one heard it fall. It's easy to think of Earth as still and unchanging. However, the fall of this natural bridge shows that Earth is always changing. Sometimes it changes overnight!

Water Works Its Way

You cannot drive or walk on a natural bridge. Natural bridges form when water or wind wears away softer rock. It leaves an arch or bridge of harder rock.

The ground around the Boulder River natural bridge is mostly limestone. As the river gradually dissolved part of the stone, a cliff formed in the riverbed. The river became a waterfall. The cliff contained some harder limestone. The flowing water slowly dissolved the softer rock over and under the harder limestone.

The ridge of harder limestone looked like a bridge. For most of the year, the waterfall flowed over and under the natural bridge. During dry weather, you could see the rocky bridge spanning the waterfall.

A Model Bridge

You can make a model of this process. Use a rubber band to fasten a piece of cloth over a pan. Put a piece of hard candy in the middle of the cloth. Cover the candy with one-half cup of white sugar. Now pour water slowly over the cloth so that it drips through into the pan. The sugar will dissolve. The hard candy will be left behind, like the natural bridge.

Water Wins!

The water continued to work away at the bridge. It flowed into cracks and dissolved more of the rock. Floods pushed against the bridge. Gradually, the bridge weakened. An aftershock from an earthquake in Idaho on July 14, 1988, may have jarred the bridge. Finally, on July 16th or 17th it fell.

Bridge? What Bridge?

If the bridge is gone, why is the site still a state monument? Even without the bridge, Natural Bridge Falls is one of the most beautiful places in Montana. In fact, steps are being taken to make it a national monument.

Most people who visit the monument want to see the waterfalls. A trail goes around the site, offering several spots where you can stop and look at the view. You can see the falls from below, above, left, and right! A wilderness trail leaves from the park.

Waterfall at the Natural Bridge State Monument with former bridge drawn in orange

Becoming a Park

Natural Bridge State Monument covers 40 acres. It hasn't always been a park. It was owned for many years by a group from nearby Big Timber, Montana. At that time, a swinging rope bridge dangled over the falls. People actually crawled out on the bridge on their stomachs. They wanted to get a more thrilling view of the waterfalls.

These activities were very risky. The Big Timber group decided to sell the land to the state of Montana in the late 1960s. The swinging bridge was quickly removed. Paths were built. Barriers on the sides discouraged anyone from climbing onto the bridge. During the construction, the entrance to the park was left unmarked. The Park Service wanted to make sure the site was safe before welcoming tourists there.

Going to Gallatin

Why should Natural Bridge become a national monument?
For one thing, it is already in Gallatin National Forest. This forest
contains almost two million acres. Much of it is wilderness.
Wilderness areas are protected from most kinds of human
disturbance. For example, roads cannot be built there.

Gallatin National Forest shares its southern border with
Yellowstone National Park. This is one of the most-visited parks in
the United States. People go to Gallatin and Yellowstone to hike,
camp, and take photographs. Eagles, turkeys, deer, moose, trout,
mountain lions, and bears are common.

Pack & Go

Natural Bridge State Monument is open all year round.
For more information, call Gallatin National Forest at
(406) 932-5155.

To get to the Natural Bridge, take Interstate 90 to Big
Timber, Montana. Big Timber is between Bozeman and
Billings. From Big Timber, take Secondary Route 298
south for 28 miles. The park will be on your left. If the
road changes to gravel, you went too far.

Consider weather and the chance of forest fires when
you plan a visit to Montana. In the Big Timber area,
temperatures seldom rise above 40 degrees in the winter.
There is lots of snow. Summers are pleasant, with cool
nights, warm days, and highs in the lower 80s. When you
go to Natural Bridge State Monument, pack good hiking
shoes. Some of the trails are steep and rugged.

Other Sites and Activities

Most people go to Montana for outdoor sports. They ski, hike, and ride horses. For more information about things to do and see, call Travel Montana at (800) 847-4868. Here are some places to consider:

- Visit the Towe Ford Museum in Deer Lodge. The museum shows Ford cars from as early as 1903. At Deer Lodge, you can also explore the history of toys. Stop at Yesterday's Playthings Doll & Toy Museum.
- Drive Going-to-the-Sun-Road in Glacier National Park. It's in the northwest corner of Montana. This road crosses the **Continental Divide** at Logan Pass. It is one of the most spectacular stretches of road in the world.
- Check out the bears at the Grizzly Discovery Center in West Yellowstone—but don't get too close! You can watch grizzly bears and gray wolves in their natural settings.
- Visit the American Computer Museum in Bozeman. Learn how the computer era began. Find out where it is likely to go in the future.

CHAPTER 8

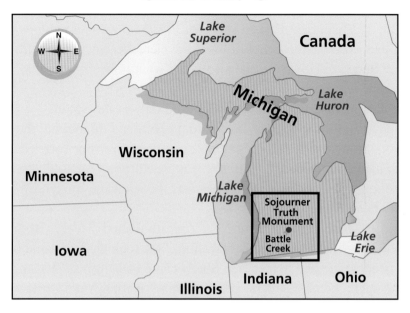

Sojourner Truth Monument
Battle Creek, Michigan

The crowded auditorium filled with applause. A tall, large-boned woman rose from her seat on the stage. As she approached the podium, her dark face broke into a smile, and the clapping got louder. She placed one hand on either side of the speaker's stand. The crowd quieted as though someone had said, "Hush!" All attention focused on the former slave at the front of the hall.

What would she say today? Would she urge them to fight for freedom for the African Americans who were still enslaved throughout the United States? Would she speak out for the rights of women to vote and own property? The speaker adjusted her bonnet that covered her crinkly, graying hair. Sojourner Truth was about to speak.

Born a Slave

Battle Creek, Michigan, honors the life and work of Sojourner Truth. At Monument Park, a statue of this great woman reminds us that the cause of freedom will live forever. In her own life, Truth knew freedom. However, she also knew what it meant not to be free. She was born into slavery in the late 1790s.

Many people think slavery happened only in the South. However, until the 1820s, slavery could be found throughout the nation. Sojourner Truth, for example, was born in New York. Her birth name was Isabella. Until she was nine or ten years old, she spoke only Dutch. At the time, this was the language spoken by many people in upstate New York.

In 1827 when the state of New York **abolished** slavery, Truth, about 30 years old, gained her freedom. She took the last name of the people who had helped her. She became Isabella Van Wagenen. Truth spent the next several years working, learning, and exploring her freedom.

Crusaded for Freedom

In 1843, Truth began traveling and speaking. She took the name of Sojourner Truth. *Sojourner* means *traveler* or *visitor*. By 1846, she had joined the abolition movement that worked to end slavery. Her height (she was nearly six feet tall), along with her powerful speaking and singing voice, commanded attention. Whenever she spoke, she sold copies of her book, *Narrative of Sojourner Truth: A Northern Slave.*

In 1851, Truth made one of her most famous speeches. In Akron, Ohio, a man in her audience stated that women were too frail to vote. Truth responded that she was strong and had worked hard, and she was a woman. She challenged the audience to see the strength and power of women. This speech is called "Ain't I a Woman?" However, no one is sure if Truth actually said, "ain't."

Sojourner Truth

During the Civil War (1861–1865), Truth helped find homes and work for freed African Americans. She pushed for schools and training for former slaves. In 1864, she was invited to meet with President Abraham Lincoln. On her way to the meeting, a horse-drawn trolley refused to pick her up because of the color of her skin. Truth raised such a protest that traffic came to a halt. She then climbed on the trolley as it was stuck in traffic!

Buried With Honor

In the late 1850s, Sojourner Truth moved to Battle Creek, Michigan. This city openly operated a station on the Underground Railroad. This railroad did not have trains. It offered safe homes, or **stations,** where enslaved people could stop on their way to Canada. (Canada outlawed slavery many years before the United States did.) Battle Creek also has a sculpture honoring its role in the Underground Railroad.

African Americans were welcome in Battle Creek. Truth bought a house there. So did some of her children and grandchildren. She continued to speak to audiences throughout the northern states. In 1883, Sojourner Truth died in Battle Creek. She is remembered for her strength and courage.

The memorial to Sojourner Truth includes a tall bronze statue by sculptor Tina Allen. Truth is buried nearby in Oak Hill Cemetery.

50

Seeing the Sojourner Sites

To explore the life of Sojourner Truth, your first stop is Monument Park. A bronze statue of Truth rises 12 feet into the air. The statue is big and bold, like the woman and her causes. You can learn more about Truth's life at the Kimball House Museum. You can also visit the Heritage of Battle Creek and Sojourner Truth Institute. This organization's goal is to preserve heritage and history.

Pack & Go

You can visit Sojourner Truth's gravesite and monument any day of the year. The Kimball House is open only on Friday afternoons and costs $2.00 for students. It is closed from January to March.

Oak Hill Cemetery is at the corner of South Avenue and Oak Hill Drive in Battle Creek. Monument Park is at the corner of Division Street and Main Street, across from City Hall. Battle Creek is on Interstate 94 between Jackson and Kalamazoo.

Call the Great Battle Creek/Calhoun County Visitor and Convention Bureau at (616) 962-2240 for more information about Sojourner Truth sites. The phone number for the Heritage of Battle Creek and Sojourner Truth Institute is (616) 965-2613.

Battle Creek has cold, snowy winters and mild summers. Make sure your clothes match the season so you'll be comfortable.

Other Sites and Activities

What else can you do in Michigan? From ice hockey, to car manufacturing, to relaxing on a quiet island, you'll keep busy. To find out more, call the Michigan Travel Bureau at (800) 543-2937. Do any of these places interest you?

- Battle Creek is home to three large cereal makers—Kellogg, Post, and Ralston Purina. You can find out all about cereal at Cereal City USA. Or come to the Cereal Festival in mid-June. You can eat at the World's Longest Breakfast Table.
- Tour the Henry Ford Museum and Greenfield Village in Dearborn. Historic buildings blend with demonstrations of crafts and trades. Of course, you can explore the history of the car.
- See the Shipwreck Historical Museum in Whitefish Point. Michigan is almost surrounded by the Great Lakes. Shipping is a major industry. Unfortunately, not all of the ships make it to port. Stories of tragic shipwrecks are told at the museum.
- Visit a replica of the Oval Office at the Gerald R. Ford Museum in Grand Rapids. It looks just as it did when President Ford was in office in the mid-1970s.
- Explore the Motown Historical Museum in Detroit. See the house where the "Motown sound" started with such famous artists as Diana Ross and the Supremes.

CHAPTER 9

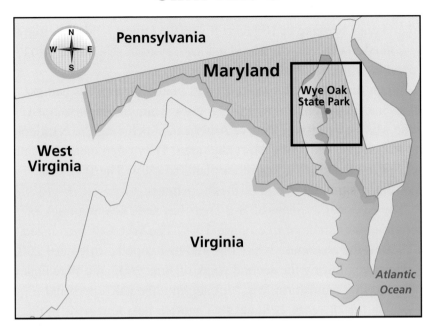

Wye Oak
Wye Mills, Maryland

Many years ago, in a clearing by the sea, an acorn bounced to the ground. Throughout the cold winter, the acorn rested in the dry grasses of the little **glade**. All around were the bare trunks of oaks, maples, beeches, and other trees of the great forest. Then the breezes began to warm, and the sun shone a little longer each day. Rain softened the ground around the acorn. Tender new leaves uncurled on the trees, and orioles called each other in the skies.

One day, with a tiny jolt, the shell of the acorn cracked. A tiny white root emerged and sought the soil. In time, two tiny leaves unfolded into the sunshine. Thus, the Wye Oak was born in the state we now call Maryland.

The Mighty Wye

What made the Wye Oak so special was its age. It was 460 years old and once towered at 100 feet. It was the largest white oak tree in the United States, and the Maryland state symbol. The distance around its trunk was 31 feet, 10 inches!

When the Wye Oak sprouted, most Native Americans had not yet seen a European. A dense forest grew from the Atlantic coast to the Mississippi River. Native Americans, including the Nanticoke and Patuxent, lived in the Maryland area. They often cleared small areas of the woods to allow other plants to grow. The Wye Oak most likely sprouted in one of these openings.

The National Register of Big Trees has been keeping track of more than 800 kinds of trees since 1940. The Wye Oak was listed in 1940 as the champion white oak and had kept the title until 2002.

However, during the second week of June 2002, the Wye Oak collapsed in a windstorm. Mr. McLaughlin, the oak's personal physician for 28 years, believes that another oak may grow in the same spot via a sucker sprout. The citizens of Maryland are keeping their fingers crossed.

Caring for the Wye Oak

Wye Oak State Park was created in Wye Mills just for this oak tree. The state bought the land around the tree so it could be protected and appreciated. The Wye Oak is Maryland's state symbol, representing strength and endurance.

A team of **arborists,** or tree specialists, took care of the Wye Oak. What do arborists do? They **fertilize** trees and spray them to keep off pests such as gypsy moths. They prune out dead limbs and tighten steel cables that protect limbs from high winds. They even went inside Wye Oak to check for diseases. A hollow space inside the tree's trunk was 10 feet high and 8 feet across. That's about the size of a bedroom!

The Wye Oak as it once looked

Making the List

How does a tree get on the National Register of Big Trees? Someone must **nominate** it and submit pictures of it. The Register also needs three measurements. It needs the height of the tree, the area over which its branches spread, and the distance around its trunk. This is measured 4.5 feet above the ground. Those three measurements give the tree a certain number of points.

To be fair, only trees of the same species are compared. For example, a champion sugar maple is 65 feet high. A champion coast redwood is 313 feet high.

Who are the "big tree hunters"? They range from people who search for champions to those who have nominated only the tree beside their home. A common bond unites them all: They love trees.

This carving was made from a limb that fell from the Wye Oak in 1984. The limb was bigger than most trees ever get. It weighed 35 tons! You can see the carving at the Department of Natural Resources in Annapolis, Maryland.

Past, Present, and Future

Trees grown from acorns of the Wye Oak connect the past and present with the future. You can order seedlings grown from these acorns. Contact the Maryland Department of Natural Resources Forest Service Tree Nursery. Of course, only your great-great-great-great-great-great grandchildren will know if your seedling becomes a grand champion!

Pack & Go

Wye Oak State Park in Wye Mills, Maryland, is open all year round. There is no charge to admire what is left of the tree. While you're there, visit the old schoolhouse next to the tree. Wye Mills, built in 1664, and Wye Church, built in 1721, are also interesting. They sound old, but they are young compared to the Wye Oak! Call (410) 820-1668 for more information.

To get to Wye Mills, take Route 50 east from Annapolis. Soon after you cross Chesapeake Bay, turn off on State Route 662 to reach Wye Oak State Park.

The Eastern Shore area of Maryland has mild winters and hot summers. The Wye Oak changed with the seasons. In its prime, the Wye Oak was green in July. In October the leaves became dark red and by May you could see the pale green of the flowering tree.

Other Activities and Sites

Maryland is a fun place to visit. You can easily get to the U.S. Capitol Building in Washington, D.C., or the U.S. Naval Academy in Annapolis. For more information, call the Maryland Office of Tourism Development at (800) 543-1036. Check out these places, too!

- Visit Babe Ruth's birthplace. At his home in Baltimore, you will learn about one of America's most famous baseball players. The Baltimore Orioles' museum is there also.
- Tour the Clara Barton National Historic Site in Washington, D.C. Barton founded the Red Cross. The site is in Barton's home. It was also the headquarters of the American Red Cross.
- See the Star Spangled Banner Flag House, also in Baltimore. This is the home of Mary Pickersgill. She sewed the flag that flew over Fort McHenry in 1814. This flag inspired our national anthem.
- In Columbia, tour the Maryland Museum of African Art. This museum displays traditional sculpture, textiles, jewelry, and musical instruments.

CHAPTER 10

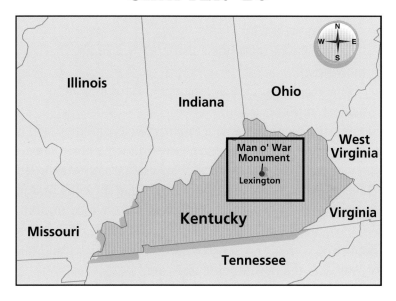

Man o' War Monument
Lexington, Kentucky

The sun shines bright on … the Kentucky Horse Park, a state park in Lexington, Kentucky. It shines on flowerbeds and well-clipped lawns, rows of stables, and rows of campers. It puts a shine on a gleaming bronze sculpture just inside the gates of the park. It glints off the water that surrounds the sculpture. Yes, the sun shines bright on the sculpture of one of the most famous horses in the world: Man o' War.

The statue is much bigger than the actual horse and is raised on a high **pedestal**. You can see it from all over the park. Still, the statue is not bigger than the memory of the horse it represents. Before you leave Man o' War, compare your **stride,** the length of one of your steps, to the stride of this great horse. At 28 feet, Man o' War's stride is hard to match, whether you are a horse or a human!

"The Mostest Horse"

> "Watching him run was like watching a living flame go down the track."

> "He was the mostest horse that ever was in all the world."

> "He is the yardstick that greatness is still measured against in horse racing."

Ask almost anyone to name a famous horse, and they will name Man o' War. Even people who have never ridden a horse or seen a race know of his greatness. Man o' War was born on March 29, 1917. Like all colts, he struggled to his feet and took his first few wobbly steps. His speed and strength were not obvious from those first moments, but Man o' War had many advantages. His parents were both strong, smart horses. His owner loved horses and raised Man o' War with the best training and care.

Man o' War grew quickly. He earned the nickname "Big Red" for his size and his red-brown coat. In 1919, Man o' War easily won his first race. In all, Man o' War ran in 21 races and won 20. In his one loss, he came in second.

Man o' War raced for only two years. To make races fair, faster horses were given weight assignments. Man o' War's weight assignment was going to be so high in his third year of racing that he would have been injured, so he was retired. However, he lived many more years, fathering another generation of racehorses. Man o' War died in 1947. He was buried in a fine oak casket lined with his black and yellow racing colors. More than 2,000 people came to pay their respects.

At the Horse Park

The statue of Man o' War at Kentucky Horse Park is almost 7 feet high at the shoulders. The real horse was about 5.5 feet tall.

60

Still, the thoroughbred Man o' War was a big horse. He weighed more than 1,000 pounds. His statue was originally erected at Faraway Farm, where he lived during the last years of his life. When Kentucky Horse Park opened, his remains were reburied there. It was fitting for the greatest, "mostest" horse to rest at a park devoted to horses.

The Kentucky Horse Park is a working farm and educational, too. You'll have fun there. You'll also leave knowing much more about horses than you did when you came. Many racing and breeding organizations have their headquarters at the park. The statue of Man o' War is a constant reminder of their mission: celebration of the horse.

Man o' War statue

"Honest Isaac" Burns Murphy

Near the memorial to Man o' War is a memorial to jockey Isaac Burns Murphy. Murphy is buried at Kentucky Horse Park because he has the highest winning percentage of any jockey ever. He won almost half of his races. Murphy was known for his honesty and for tight finishes, called *murfinishes*. He would urge his horse just far enough ahead to win by a nose!

Murphy was born in Kentucky in 1861. He worked with horses even as a boy. At age 15, he won his first horse race. Three times, he won the Kentucky Derby, one of the most famous races in the world. He died in 1896. In 1967, his grave was moved so that the famous jockey and the famous horse could be honored together. In 1977, both graves were moved to the new Kentucky Horse Park.

Jockey Isaac Burns Murphy

All About Horses

At the Kentucky Horse Park, you can visit the International Museum of the Horse. It traces the history of the horse. Other exhibits include horses of the Civil War and racing costumes. You can also admire equine art. *Equine* means "horse." This art includes paintings, sculptures, drawings, and photographs related to horses.

In the museum, you can learn about 100 breeds of horse. For example, huge workhorses, such as Clydesdales, can weigh as much as a ton each. Fully grown Shetland ponies can weigh as little as 300 pounds.

Pack & Go

At the Kentucky Horse Park, you can also camp, watch horse parades, and tour the farm. The admission charge depends on the time of year and your age. From March to October, the park is open every day. From November through February, it is closed on Mondays and Tuesdays. Call the park at (800) 678-8813 for more information.

To get to the Man o' War Monument, take Exit 120 off Interstate 75. The exit is just a few miles north of Lexington.

Winters are mild in the Lexington area. Summers are hot and sunny. Check a local weather report before you travel. Take sunscreen and maybe a bottle of water. You'll be doing a lot of walking, so wear comfortable shoes.

Other Activities and Sites

Kentucky is a place of history and natural beauty. Call the Kentucky Department of Travel Development at (800) 225-8747 for information. Find out more about these places of interest:

- The National Scouting Museum is in Murray. You can follow the history of scouting since it began in 1910. You can also try your strength and teamwork at an outdoor ropes course.
- Visit the National Corvette Museum in Bowling Green. You can see a model from every year that this sports car has been made. You can also tour the manufacturing plant. It's the only factory where Corvettes are made.
- The Abraham Lincoln Birthplace National Historic Site is in Hodgenville. It includes a cabin like the one in which Lincoln was born. The cabin is inside a marble memorial. There are 56 steps up to the door, symbolizing the 56 years of Lincoln's life.
- Mammoth Cave National Park near Cave City has more than 300 miles of caves. A visit during the summer is a good way to cool off. The caves stay at about 54 degrees all year round.
- Go to Paducah for the American Quilters Society Show and Contest. It celebrates the Appalachian art of quilting. The show is held every April.

CHAPTER 11

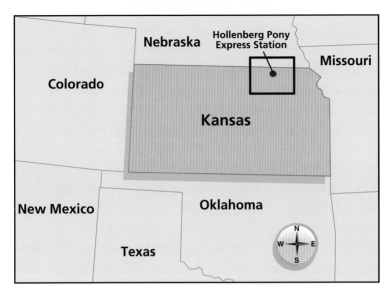

Hollenberg Pony Express Station
Hanover, Kansas

The woman pushed her hair back from her damp forehead and scanned the horizon. She was bouncing on the hard wooden seat of the covered wagon. Her eyes followed the sun as it set in the west. There it was! She could see a group of buildings. At last! A place to get a hot meal she hadn't cooked herself. A chance to rest the oxen and repair the wagon. On the horizon, she could see the Hollenberg Pony Express Station.

Her family was walking beside the wagon, but before she could call to them, a shout went up behind them. Then she heard the thunder of a galloping horse. The horse and its rider flashed past, easily overtaking the lumbering wagon. As it disappeared toward Hollenberg Station, the woman smiled to herself. The Pony Express rider would be long gone to his next station by the time her family got there!

At the Station

Hollenberg Station was founded in 1858. Gerat Hollenberg, a German **immigrant,** built it to meet the needs of travelers on the Oregon Trail. In the mid-1800s, European people from the eastern United States started moving West in large numbers. They were spurred on when gold was discovered in California in 1849.

The journey west was hard. The pioneers traveled in wooden wagons pulled by oxen. Oxen were stronger and tougher than horses. They could go longer without water and could keep their footing in deep mud and on steep slopes. The wagons usually had canvas stretched over a frame, making them tents on wheels. A group of wagons traveling together was called a wagon train.

Hollenberg located his station on a branch of the Oregon-California Trail. He had fresh horses for stagecoaches. He had food for people and corn and grain to feed their livestock. They could buy a new ox or cow. They could get their wagons fixed. They could also stock up on supplies to build a new home at the end of their trip.

Hollenberg Station also served as an inn. Hollenberg's wife, Sophia, ran this part of the station. Travelers could get a hot meal, a room, and a much-needed bath. The trail was dry and dusty. Water was used for drinking, cooking, and watering animals, not washing!

The station began as a log cabin. Additions made room for overnight guests and dining. Barns and sheds sprouted to stable animals and store supplies. To travel-weary pioneers, Hollenberg Station was a welcome sight.

Here Comes the Pony Express!

Hollenberg Station was well established by 1860, so it was a good choice for a Pony Express stop. The Pony Express began that year. Wagon trains took many months to carry mail from Missouri to California. The Pony Express guaranteed to do it in ten days! The Express stations were 10 to 15 miles apart.

The stationmaster's job was to have a fresh horse saddled and ready to go at just the right time. The Pony Express rider would come flying in on his horse. He would jump off his tired horse, grab a drink of water, and jump on the fresh horse. No time was lost in the transfer from one horse to another.

The Hollenberg Pony Express Station stands where it stood during the days of the Pony Express.

Illustration of Pony Express rider

Small, Strong, Brave, and Orphaned

The Pony Express wanted small riders. They wouldn't wear out the horses. The riders had to be strong enough to ride 75 miles at a stretch. Because the job was so dangerous, the Express preferred riders with no families. That way, if something happened to a rider, no one was left behind to grieve.

The riders rode fast over the same rutted ground that broke wagon axles. They rode hard over the same mud that stopped oxen in their tracks. They rode through snow, sleet, storms, and heat. The mail had to go through! The fastest delivery was President Lincoln's inaugural speech in 1861. It reached Sacramento, California, in just seven days.

The Pony Express didn't last very long. By November 1861, telegraph wires reached from coast to coast. Messages could be sent instantly, so the Pony Express went out of business. However, the courage and daring of the riders had already become legend.

End of an Era, End of a Station

The telegraph ended the Pony Express. Soon after, in May of 1869, a golden spike connected the two parts of the nation's first transcontinental railroad. A train now crossed the United States. Few people still traveled the Oregon Trail. Trains were quicker, safer, and more comfortable.

The Hollenberg Station shut down in the mid-1860s. Several buildings were torn down or abandoned. In 1941, the state of Kansas bought the main building. It was made into a state historic site. You can still tour the original log cabin and its additions. You can learn about the dramatic years of the Oregon Trail and the Pony Express.

Pack & Go

The Hollenberg Station State Historic Site is open from 10:00 A.M. to 5:00 P.M., Wednesday through Saturday. Its hours are 1:00 P.M. to 5:00 P.M. on Sunday. Call to double-check the times. The phone number is (785) 337-2635. Admission is $2 for adults and $1 for children.

To get to Hanover, take U.S. Route 75 north from Topeka. Then go west on U.S. Route 36. The Station is four miles north of U.S. 36 on State Route 243. Stop and visit the Potawatomi and Kickapoo Indian Reservations on your way.

This part of Kansas has cold winters and hot, hot summers. Sudden changes, including violent storms, are common. Stay tuned to the weather report.

Other Activities and Sites

The wide, open spaces of Kansas mean long distances between towns. Still, there are many things to see and do. Near the Hollenberg Pony Express Station, you can see the world's first bulldozer. It was built in 1923. You can also visit the Haddam Jail, built in 1901. To find out more about Kansas attractions, call the Travel and Tourism Development Division at (800) 252-6727.

- The Amelia Earhart Birthplace Museum is in Atchison. Earhart was a famous pilot in the early years of flying. She broke many records. The museum hosts a festival every July.
- The Barbed Wire Museum is in La Crosse. You can learn how twisted wire fenced in the great open spaces of the American West. Many kinds of barbed wire are on display.
- See a rebuilt "Little House on the Prairie" in Independence. The cabin is built on the site where Laura Ingalls Wilder lived from 1869 to 1871.
- The geographic center of the United States (not counting Alaska and Hawaii) is near Lebanon. To be in the middle of it all, stand next to the monument that marks this spot.

Did you enjoy your trip? Where are you going next? The places in this book are just the beginning. There's a big, wide country out there for you to explore. When you're done with that, there's a big, wide world waiting to be discovered. All you have to do is Pack & Go!

GLOSSARY

abolished (uh•**bol**•ishd) got rid of

anthropologists (an•thruh•**pol**•uh•jists) scientists who study ancient people and their lives

arborists (**ar**•buhr•ists) tree specialists

aviation (ay•vee•**ay**•shuhn) the operation of aircraft

aviator (**ay**•vee•ay•tuhr) a person who operates an aircraft; a pilot

civil rights (**siv**•uhl **ryts**) the rights of a citizen

constitution (kon•sti•**too**•shuhn) the basic laws and principles of a nation

Continental Divide (kon•tuh•**nehn**•tuhl di•**vyd**) a point in the mountains of the western United States where rivers on one side flow west and rivers on the other side flow east or south

dictator (**dik**•tay•tuhr) a leader who holds all the power

economy (i•**kon**•uh•mee) the flow of money and products in an area

fertilize (**fur**•tuhl•yz) to provide food and nutrients to plants

glade (**glayd**) an open space surrounded by woods

herald (**hehr**•uhld) one who announces or foreshadows an event

immigrant (**im**•i•gruhnt) a person who comes to a country to live

integrated (**in**•ti•gray•tid) including all groups of people in schools and other institutions

kindling (**kind**•ling) small twigs and sticks used to start a fire

manure (muh•**nur**) waste material from animals

nominate (**nom**•uh•nayt) to name; to suggest for an honor or office

pedestal (**pehd**•i•stuhl) the supporting base of a statue

restored (ri•**stord**) returned a building or object to an earlier condition

sandbars (**sand**•barz) ridges of sand built up by water currents

stations (**stay**•shuhnz) resting places

stride (**stryd**) the length of one step

surveying (suhr•**vay**•ing) determining boundary lines

Tejanos (tay•**hah**•nohs) Mexican citizens of Texas before it became a state; their descendants

unkempt (un•**kehmpt**) disorderly; not neat; uncombed

winter solstice (**win**•tuhr **sol**•stis) the shortest day of the year in the Northern Hemisphere

PACK and GO INDEX